Foreword

Robert Ripley began his career as a sports cartoonist. One day, he was facing a deadline and couldn't think of anything to draw. Then he had a brainstorm. Digging through his files, Ripley found nine amazing sports facts—and finished his cartoon just in time. Little did he know it would become the first of thousands of Believe It or Not! cartoons.

Over the years, Ripley broadened the scope of his column, including many different subjects besides sports. He became interested in all kinds of oddities—people, places, things, and events. He traveled all over the world in search of astounding phenomena to share with his readers. Books and syndicated newspaper columns include his material in the form of Believe It or Not! cartoons. Museums called Odditoriums display a wide range of things he collected. The Ripley archives encompass the astounding collection that was Robert Ripley's passion.

Animals were always a favorite topic of Ripley's, so it is not surprising that the archives are filled with entries about creatures of all kinds. Inspired by this dynamic collection, Wild World books give readers an up-close view of the living beings that share our Earth. Among the most intriguing animals are amphibians and reptiles. Their ancestors appeared on Earth more than 300 million years ago. The unique adaptations that these creatures made to their environments mean that descendants of these animals roam our planet today.

Imagine a mother frog that holds her unborn young in her stomach and gives birth to them through her mouth. Picture geckos that can travel across walls and ceilings—upside down—gripping the surface with their special feet. Think about snakes lying on the ground, with their tongues hanging out, "playing dead" in order to protect themselves from predators. These and many more surprises await you in the pages of this book.

The colorful photographs, amazing facts, and original cartoons from the Ripley's archive collected in *Cold-Blooded Creatures* will give you a glimpse of these unique and fascinating animals.

`Prepare to dive into the astonishing world of amphibians and reptiles.`

Madeline Boskey, Ph.D.
Series Editor

Introduction

I grew up with a special advantage for a budding herpetologist. My family lived in the country, and we even had a pond in our front yard. It was a rather small pond, but it was a perfect laboratory for a young naturalist. I spent many happy hours alongside that pond observing (and trying to catch!) the creatures that made their homes there. Frogs, turtles, an occasional water snake, and rarely, a salamander or two made appearances. In back of the house were a few acres of prairie, an area with its own set of animals that were different from those that lived by or in the pond. There was a hedge in back, near a ravine, where I could nearly always find box turtles. This was also where garter snakes and the occasional kingsnake could be most easily found. So by the time I was about 10 years old, I had already begun to have an intuitive understanding of the relationship between a habitat and the animals that make their homes within it.

Like any kid, I was also fascinated by animals that were unusual—maybe even a bit weird. Large and frightening animals definitely captured my interest. Trips to the zoo and the library added to my knowledge. I decided that Komodo dragons were definitely cool. They are big, fast, and possess a bite that gives a nasty infection even if it doesn't kill. Poison dart frogs were among my favorite animals because they are so colorful and have a toxin in their skin. I was also intrigued by the all-female species of lizards. Yes, there was definitely enough weirdness in the world of amphibians and reptiles to satisfy my taste for the exotic.

At college, I began to discover what we really know about biology and, more important, how much we still don't know. I was amazed to discover how many new species of amphibians and reptiles are named every year. I also found there were many interesting and still-unanswered questions about amphibians and reptiles. The evolutionary biologist Ernst Mayr famously divided the questions biologists ask into how questions and why questions. How questions ask about the mechanism responsible for some biological process, for example, how does a tadpole metamorphose into a frog? Why questions ask about the conditions that are responsible for the process existing in the first place. We have a decent understanding of the how questions for only a handful of amphibian and reptile species. We know about amphibian development, for example, almost entirely from one frog and one salamander species. As for why questions, we have some knowledge about species in the best-explored areas of the world but know almost nothing about many species. So there are still many discoveries waiting to be made about amphibians and reptiles.

This book makes me remember my own initial discoveries about herpetology and  the books that kept me interested in these wonderful animals. You might even get hooked on herpetology and decide to make a career of it. Stranger things have happened!

David Dickey
Herpetologist
American Museum of Natural History

Cold-Blooded CREATURES

Written by:
Michele Sobel Spirn

With an Introduction by:
David Dickey
Department of Herpetology
American Museum of Natural History

Series Edited by:
Madeline Boskey, Ph.D.

SCHOLASTIC INC.

New York   Toronto   London   Auckland   Sydney
Mexico City   New Delhi   Hong Kong   Buenos Aires

Developed by Nancy Hall, Inc., New York, NY
Designed by Gen Shibuya and Tom Koken

Original art by Ron Zalme

No part of this publication may be reproduced in whole or in part, or stored in a retrieval system, or transmitted in any form or by any means, electronic, mechanical, photocopying, recording, or otherwise, without written permission by the publisher.

Published by Scholastic Inc.,
90 Old Sherman Turnpike, Danbury, Connecticut 06816

Copyright © 2004 by Ripley Entertainment Inc. Ripley's, Ripley's Believe It or Not!, Believe It or Not!, and Believe It! are registered trademarks of Ripley Entertainment Inc.

All rights reserved.

SCHOLASTIC and associated logos are trademarks and/or registered trademarks of Scholastic Inc.

Printed in the U.S.A.
First Scholastic printing, April 2004
ISBN 0-439-63362-1

Contents

Creeping Creatures 2

Astounding Amphibians 4

Frogs and Toads 8

Salamanders and Newts 15

Remarkable Reptiles 19

Crocodiles 24

Alligators! 29

Turtles and Tortoises 33

Sensational Snakes 38

Lizards 43

Lore and Legend 54

More about Cold-Blooded Creatures 55

Glossary 56

Index 58

Creeping Creatures

Ancient Animals

Amphibians and reptiles are perhaps the most misunderstood members of the animal kingdom. They are often feared by humans. Those people who take the time to find out about them will find they are fascinating creatures. The first amphibians and reptiles appeared on Earth well over 300 million years ago. Many reptiles and some amphibians were particularly adaptable, so many of today's species resemble their ancestors from long ago.

Today, these creatures play an important role within the food chain. They help to keep insects, small mammals, and even some other reptile and amphibian populations under control.

The red-eyed tree frog is aptly named. It is a tree dweller.

Amphibian vs. Reptile

Some people think that reptiles and amphibians are similar, but they are actually two distinct groups of cold-blooded vertebrates. In fact, there are many differences between them.

Scientists have described more than 5,000 species of amphibians from all over the world. At least 230 of those species live in the United States. Amphibians include frogs, toads, and salamanders. The skin of amphibians is moist and is not covered with scales. Many amphibians secrete poisons to ward off enemies. They lay jellylike eggs in the water. Amphibians go through metamorphosis, evolving from a larval to an adult form.

The Natal green snake is native to Africa.

Creeping Creatures

The desert horned lizard has long scales on its toes that help it move through sand.

Well over 8,000 species of reptiles have been catalogued by scientists. These animals, including snakes, turtles, lizards, and crocodiles, lay their eggs on land or give birth to live young. Their skin is dry and covered with scales. Reptiles do not undergo metamorphosis. Their young look quite a lot like the adults they will become.

Scientists from the Department of Fish and Wildlife study eastern box turtles.

Astounding Amphibians

Two Lives to Live

The ornate horned frog is a native of South America. It lives in burrows in tropical forests.

Picture the Earth of 360 million years ago. There is more water than land. The oceans teem with all kinds of fish and sea animals. Then some of the sea animals crawl out of the water and onto land. To help them live better on land, their fins turn into legs. These new animals become used to living on land but still like to be near water. Since they live the first part of their lives in water and the second part on land, they are called amphibians—from the Greek words *amphi* and *bios*, which mean "double life."

Astounding Amphibians

The red hills salamander lives in burrows on the shady side of steep hills. It is found only in one area of southern Alabama.

Chilling Out

Today, there are more than 5,000 species of amphibians. These include frogs, toads, salamanders, and caecilians. Caecilians are wormlike creatures that live in the tropics. All amphibians are vertebrates—they have a backbone—and are cold-blooded. Unlike humans, who are warm-blooded, an amphibian's body temperature changes with its surroundings. If you put a frog on top of a scoop of ice cream, its body temperature will drop to echo the ice cream's chill. Similarly, if a frog hopped onto a plate of hot french fries, its body temperature would rise.

Generally, amphibians prefer cool, moist areas. They tend to avoid hot, dry places. Many hang out near ponds, swamps, in grasslands, and in rain forests, where they can be near water and the temperature is consistent. A few species live in deserts. In Australia's dry outback, burrowing frogs live by breeding and feeding only during the area's rare rainstorms.

Common toads usually dwell in forests or fields. They sometimes hang around near human habitations.

A herpetologist is someone who studies amphibians and reptiles. The word comes from the Greek *herpeto*—meaning "creeping things"—and *logia*—meaning "study or knowledge."

The Skin They're In

Amphibians go naked. They have no hair, feathers, or scales. Their skin is extremely important to amphibians. While some amphibians breathe through their lungs, like humans do, they also take in oxygen through their skin. A slimy mucous layer protects their skin covering and keeps it from drying out.

Most amphibians don't drink water because they get enough moisture through their skin. If their bodies need more water, it is absorbed through the skin. Likewise, if their bodies have excess water, it is released through the skin.

Rough-skin newts have warty skin. Their undersides range from yellow to orange.

Contrary to what some people think, a person cannot get warts from touching a toad's skin.

Most frogs have smooth, moist skin.

Toads tend to have dry, warty skin.

Morphing Inside and Out

Astounding Amphibians

How do amphibians change into full-grown animals? Take the frog, for example. The frog starts as a larva, called a tadpole, a tiny creature that looks somewhat like a fish and lives in water. A tadpole has gills to breathe underwater. It has a wide mouth and tiny teeth to feed on microscopic plants. On each side it has two little nubs, which eventually become legs. The tadpole also develops lungs and begins to gulp in air at the water's surface. Its tail begins to disappear as it grows older.

Other amazing changes are going on inside the tadpole's body as well. A wall of tissue splits the heart from two chambers into three. This makes it easier for the blood to move between the heart and the tadpole's new lungs. Its intestines are shrinking, its mouth is widening, and its very small teeth will be replaced by larger teeth. These transformations will help the adult frog catch and digest its mostly insect diet.

Finally, the tadpole climbs out of the water to make its home on land. It is now a full-grown frog. Depending on what kind of frog it is, the entire metamorphosis can take anywhere from less than two weeks to a few months.

The Pacific giant salamander has smooth, shiny skin.

Frogs and Toads

Common toads, which are found in northwest Africa and Asia, actually walk rather than hop.

The sucker pads on the end of each toe help red-eyed tree frogs stick to branches.

Red-eyed tree frogs are great jumpers.

Frogs Get Around

Frogs are the most widespread of the amphibians. They live almost everywhere except in the polar regions. Usually, frogs live near water and have smooth skin, long hind legs, and fully webbed feet. Many frogs are great jumpers. Wallace's flying frogs in Southeast Asia have feet that are heavily webbed so they can spread them and glide away from their enemies.

Gulf coast toads live in cities and towns. They sometimes gather under streetlights to feed on insects.

What's the Difference?

Frogs and toads are both members of the same group, the tail-less amphibians, or Anura. The animals we customarily call frogs are those that live mostly in water. As a rule, they have smooth, moist skin and relatively long limbs that make them good jumpers. The animals usually called toads are found in damp areas on land. They typically have rough, dry skin, relatively short limbs, and don't jump as well as frogs. Many different families of Anurans have both frog and toad species, so many scientists simply call them all frogs when it is unimportant to emphasize the difference.

Frogs and Toads

White's tree frogs are nocturnal creatures.

River frogs have big eyes that help them find food and avoid enemies.

The ornate horned frog is fat and colorful. Because of its huge mouth, it is sometimes called the Pac-Man frog.

Froggy Vision

Frogs need good vision to catch fast-flying insects. Typically, they have eyes that bulge and can see in almost any direction. Even when the light is dim, frogs can see clearly. Some frogs have third eyelids, called nictitating membranes, which they can draw across the eye to protect it while still being able to see a little of what's going on. Their eyes are on top of their heads, so frogs can sit in the water with only their eyes and noses above the surface.

These big red eyes may startle potential predators.

Some frogs and toads shed their skin once a week. Guess what some species do with the old skin? They eat it!

A frog's eyes help it swallow! When a frog swallows a fly, its eyes sink through the openings in its skull and help force the insect down its throat. That's why a frog looks like it's blinking when it eats.

Frogs and Toads

The male green tree frog makes a loud noise that sounds like a quacking duck.

Stay Tuned to WFROG

Frogs are music makers. Besides making croaking sounds, they whistle, twitter, chirp, trill, and scream. Usually, it is the male frogs that are serenading the females. Large frogs have deep voices. Small ones have higher croaks.

Is Anyone Listening?

The outer ears of most frogs consist of circular tympanums. The hearing ability of frogs and toads varies from species to species, depending upon the size of their ears. Female frogs and toads may be "tuned" to hear certain frequencies more than others. This means that females can hear males of the same species easily, ultimately helping them to mate.

Of all amphibians, frogs have the best sense of hearing.

A horned frog's mouth accounts for more than half of its body length. That's why this frog is sometimes called a mouth on legs.

The round spot visible just behind the eye is the tympanum. The orange-eyed tree frog has the reputation of being loud.

Some White's tree frogs have lived as long as 20 years.

Frogs and Toads

A Frog Is Born

The result of a frog's love song is mating. The male climbs onto the female's back and clasps her with his legs. As she lays her eggs, the male releases his sperm and fertilizes the eggs. All amphibian eggs are covered with a soft, jellylike substance. Some frogs lay their eggs in clusters, called spawn, while others deposit their eggs in long chains.

One frog, the gastric brooding frog, actually gives birth to its young through its mouth. The mother eats the eggs, which then live and hatch in her stomach. As the tadpoles grow, the mother's stomach expands until it takes up most of her body. Some of these frogs hold up to 30 babies in their stomachs. After eight weeks, the mother gives birth by opening her mouth. The tadpoles gradually leave. If a tadpole doesn't leave the mother's mouth, the mother frog swallows it again, and it is born later.

Some South American frogs lay their eggs on tree branches near water. As the eggs hatch, the tadpoles drop into the water.

When it is mating time, male Pacific tree frogs call out to females in loud choruses.

The mating ritual of blue poison dart frogs includes chasing and wrestling.

11

Frogs and Toads

Danger!

Although frogs may lay hundreds of eggs, the odds are against most of the young surviving and hatching into tadpoles. Why? Ducks, fish, and insects may eat the eggs. Water scorpions, newts, water beetles, and crayfish can devour the tadpoles. The pond in which they hatch can dry up.

Tinker reed frogs are extremely numerous and have loud calls that sound like the word tack.

Poison!

Frogs and toads have many enemies, but they can protect themselves. All frogs and toads have poison glands in their skin. The most lethal are the poison dart frogs, such as the blue poison dart frog, which lives in the rain forests of Central and South America. They are called poison dart frogs because the Chocó Indians of Colombia coat the tip of each of their hunting arrows with the frogs' poison.

The blue poison dart frog prefers to live in dark, moist, tropical rain forests.

Some toads have enlarged glands, one behind each eye. These glands contain a white poison. If the toad is threatened, the poisonous fluid oozes out. If the poison gets in the eyes or mouth of the attacker, it causes a burning sensation. Some toads, such as the Colorado River toad found in the western United States and the cane toad of South America, have stronger poisons that can cause muscle spasms, irregular heartbeats, and breathing problems for their enemies.

The African bullfrog is highly aggressive. It can inflict a serious bite.

A Frog's Worst Friend

Humans pose a great threat to frogs and toads. The oils in our skin are bad for them. The animals' fragile skin can be destroyed if people pick them up. Frogs and toads are also affected by climate changes, such as global warming, and destruction of their habitats. When rain forests are destroyed and marshy areas are built up and filled in, frogs and toads lose their homes. Frogs are also vulnerable to water and air pollution because their skin absorbs water and oxygen.

Frogs and Toads

The leaf-folding frog breeds during rainy seasons.

The golden poison dart frog, only 0.5 to 2 inches (1.25 to 5.08 cm) long, contains enough poison in its skin to kill 10 people.

The waxy tree frog produces a waxy substance on its skin that helps it retain moisture.

13

Frogs and Toads

Frog Alert

Frogs and toads are indicator species. This means they are the first to be affected by changes in the environment. Unfortunately, over the past 20 to 30 years, some kinds of amphibians around the world have been dying out. Scientists believe that the deaths of these species may be an advance warning to us that the environment is becoming unhealthy for humans.

Frogs and toads eat insects and keep the pest population down. Frogs are often used in medical research. Recently, chemicals extracted from the skin of South American frogs led to the discovery of a powerful painkiller.

While the red-eyed tree frog is not endangered, the environment it lives in is shrinking.

AN **AUSTRALIAN FROG** (Cheiroleptes Platycephalus), AWARE THAT A DROUGHT IS PENDING, FILLS UP WITH WATER UNTIL IT SWELLS LIKE A BALLOON. THE FROG THEN SLEEPS FOR AS LONG AS 18 MONTHS.

The tomato frog of Madagascar has the shape and color of a tomato. When it is frightened, it puffs itself up to make predators think it's too big to swallow.

Hidden from View: Salamanders and Newts

Newts to You

Fire belly, hellbender, mud puppy, devil dog, red-spotted—all are kinds of salamanders. Salamanders may look a lot like lizards with their long bodies and tails that are nearly half their body lengths. Salamanders, however, have no scales, and most have smooth, moist skin. Some salamanders are called newts.

As adults, most newts spend more time in the water than salamanders. For example, red-spotted newts are born in water. Then they spend two or three years on land, where they are called efts and are orange-red in color. Finally, they return to the water for the rest of their lives. There, they turn green and develop broad tails that help them swim.

Like many newts, the skin of the California newt contains glands that secrete poisons. So, look but don't touch these creatures.

Gender differences are usually greater in newts than in salamanders, and their courtship behavior is generally more complicated.

The male newt may dance around the female in a circle in the water. He also releases chemicals called pheromones from the cloaca (the rear end of the digestive system) at the base of his tail. He waves the scent toward the female with his tail to attract her before leaving a capsule of sperm. The female retrieves the sperm with her cloaca to fertilize her eggs.

The male salamander releases pheromones from a gland under his chin and deposits them on the female's nose. This gland is active only during mating time.

THE EUROPEAN SALAMANDER CAN GROW NEW LENSES ON ITS EYES IF THE OLD LENSES ARE REMOVED.

Salamanders and Newts

A Salamander Tale

Salamanders are the only amphibians that have long tails as adults. If an enemy threatens it, a salamander can shed its tail. When the tail is discarded, it flops around on the ground and distracts the predator. Often, a salamander can slip away and grow a new tail later.

The hatched young of the yellow-eyed salamander look like small adults.

The first salamanders lived about 150 million years ago.

Water Babies

Salamanders are cold-blooded. Some live only in water, some part-time in water, and some solely on cool, forested land. Most newts commute between land and watery environments near streams or springs.

If salamanders or newts are born in the water, their larvae develop external gills and teeth. During metamorphosis, most salamanders lose their gills and acquire lungs. For some, this process takes two or three months. For others, it takes up to five years. Some salamanders, however, never lose their gills because they never leave the water.

Salamanders and Newts

Night Life

During the day, salamanders hide under logs, in moist areas, or deep under the water. They hunt for food in the cool, dark hours of night. Those that live on land enjoy munching on insects, slugs, and worms. Instead of stalking their prey, they sit and wait for it to come to them. When a juicy worm comes into view, salamanders roll out their fleshy, sticky tongues and snatch it up. Salamanders that live in the water locate their food by smell. They open their mouths and suck in snails, tadpoles, and small fish.

Arboreal salamanders dine on slugs and snails.

Some captive salamanders have lived for more than 50 years.

Salamanders and Newts

Hellbenders like to be left alone. If two hellbenders meet, they may fight and if one is bigger than the other, the larger one may eat the smaller.

The slender salamander has a wormlike body—and legs!

These Puppies Don't Bark

Mud puppies are salamanders that live their whole lives in water. They got their name because they live down in the muddy bottoms of rivers or streams, and people once believed they could bark. However, the truth is that salamanders usually remain silent except for an occasional click, snap, or yelp. Hellbenders, another type of salamander, also make their homes in water and can grow quite large. The biggest hellbender ever recorded was nearly 2.5 feet (0.76 m) long. In China and Japan, hellbender relatives have reached lengths of more than 5 feet (1.52 m). Hellbenders got their name because some people imagined they were as ugly as monsters from hell.

Today, there are about 380 species of salamanders.

Homebodies

Most land salamanders do not travel more than 1 mile (1.6 km) in their entire lifetimes. Some scientists estimate that at least 50 percent of land salamanders die because the spots they have settled in are too cold for them. Yet they stay rather than move to better, warmer places.

REMARKABLE REPTILES

Living Fossils

Some scientists call reptiles "living fossils" because of their long history on Earth. The earliest known reptiles existed 338 million years ago. They looked like a cross between a crocodile and a lizard. Early reptiles were very different from the animals we know today. There were doglike creatures called *Cynognathus*, which were about 7 feet (2.13 m) long and covered with hair. Giant sea lizards known as mosasaurs filled the oceans—they grew to about 49 feet (14.9 m) long. *Rhamphorhynchus*, pterosaurs or flying reptiles, launched themselves from cliffs and glided through the air.

Today, there are four main groups of reptiles: crocodilians, lizards and snakes, turtles and tortoises, and the tuatara. They are all cold-blooded vertebrates. All have scales on their skin and young that hatch from eggs.

Remarkable Reptiles

A reptile active during the daytime has eyes with round pupils, while those active at night have slitlike pupils.

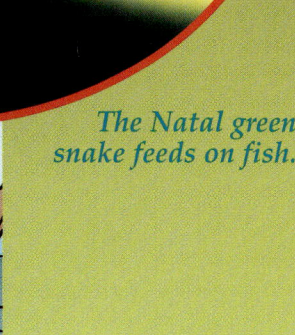

The Natal green snake feeds on fish.

They may look fearsome, but Galápagos marine iguanas are harmless. They feed on algae that grow on rocks by the shore.

The Reptile That Helped Darwin

In 1835, the naturalist Charles Darwin was working on his famous studies of animals. While he was standing on the shore of the Galápagos Islands about 600 miles (966 km) off the Pacific coast of South America, he noticed a large lizard crawling on the rocks. Some impulse made Darwin grab the lizard by its tail and throw it into the sea. The lizard swam back to shore. Darwin became interested. He threw the lizard back into the sea again and again. The lizard, now known as the Galápagos marine iguana, was able to swim very well, but it refused to stay in the water. It kept returning to the shore, even though Darwin would just throw it back into the sea.

Later, Darwin wrote that he suspected that the reptile had no enemy on shore, while it was prey to sharks in the sea. He thought that probably because of its "fixed and hereditary instinct," the lizard behaved as if the shore was a safe place, regardless of what actually happened there. So even if there was an enemy on shore and the sea was safe for the lizard, the lizard would still head back to shore because it believed that the shore had always been safe.

Keeping Warm

Darwin was right about reptiles and other animals seeking safety. The marine iguana was also looking for warmth. Warmth is extremely important to all reptiles, and they are constantly changing their environments to maintain their proper temperatures. If a reptile is cold, it will move into the sun and may flatten its body to increase the area exposed to the warmth. Some reptiles may actually darken their skin if they feel a chill so they can absorb more sunlight. Dark colors soak up more radiant heat than lighter colors. A good portion of a reptile's life is spent moving from warm spots to cool places and back again to maintain a constant body temperature.

Remarkable Reptiles

If its body temperature is not warm enough, a reptile that has just eaten may die from starvation because it can't digest its food.

Leopard lizards prefer flat areas rather than dense brush or grass that interferes with their running.

It's a Boy! It's a Girl!

Scientists have even discovered that the sex of some kinds of turtle and alligator babies is determined by how warm the nest holding the eggs is. For example, in a particular population, if the temperature is lower than 86 degrees from 7 to 21 days after the reptile lays the eggs, the hatchlings will be female. If the temperature is higher than 93.2 degrees, the babies will be male.

The habitat of the American alligator includes marshes, rivers, and swamps of the southeastern United States.

Remarkable Reptiles

Fighting for Love

The courtship of reptiles can be violent at times. At the start of the breeding season, a male lizard wrestles with other males for a particular female. However, a weaker male will generally give up the fight before he gets hurt. Other reptiles take a more gentle approach. A male snake rubs his chin along the back of a female snake and wraps his tail around hers when mating. Also, a male tuatara walks in slow circles around the female. If she likes him, she will permit him to mate with her. Otherwise, she'll disappear into her burrow.

A pair of agama lizards.

A female Morelet's crocodile typically builds a nest of twigs and rotting vegetation. She lays up to three dozen eggs.

22

Remarkable Reptiles

Scientists collect Kemp's Ridley sea turtle eggs.

Eggs-tra, Eggs-tra

Some lizards and snakes give birth to live young, but most lay eggs that have shells. Female alligators build mounds of mud and rotting plant life, and remain with their eggs until they hatch. The heat produced by the decaying mound and the sun incubates the eggs, and they hatch after two to three months. Rattlesnakes keep their eggs inside their bodies until the young hatch and emerge. Crocodiles and pythons protect the eggs and the nest, but turtles lay their eggs and leave before they are hatched.

Fencing protects the habitat of desert tortoises.

The secretary bird of Africa hunts tortoises, turtles, and snakes. It stamps its feet to flush the reptiles out of the grass.

Enemies All Around

Baby reptiles face tremendous odds against surviving their first months of life. They are the favorite prey of many birds, snakes, mammals, and sharks. Most animals, however, avoid poisonous snakes.

A RATTLESNAKE CAN INFLICT A BITE UP TO AN HOUR AFTER ITS HEAD HAS BEEN CUT OFF!

23

Crocodiles

CROCODILES

When SuperCroc Ruled the Earth

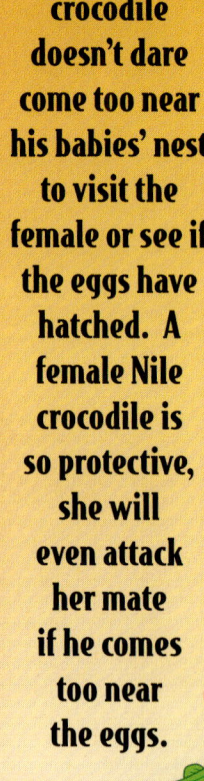

The male Nile crocodile doesn't dare come too near his babies' nest to visit the female or see if the eggs have hatched. A female Nile crocodile is so protective, she will even attack her mate if he comes too near the eggs.

Crocodiles and alligators are the only remaining archosaurs. This group, sometimes called "ruling reptiles," included the dinosaurs. While crocodiles have been living on Earth for more than 250 million years, paleontologists have discovered that one of the largest crocodiles of all time lived 110 million years ago. Named *Sarcosuchus imperator*, or "flesh crocodile emperor," this creature has been nicknamed SuperCroc. It was at least 40 feet (12.19 m) long—as long as a city bus—and weighed about 10 tons (9,072 kg).

The SuperCroc fossils were discovered in Niger, Africa, in a hot, sandy area. A nearly complete 6-foot-long (1.8-m) skull and other remains were found. When SuperCroc lived there, the country was filled with rivers, and this emperor of the reptiles prowled the riverbanks, crunching fish and other creatures in its enormous jaws.

Crocodiles cool down by lying in chilly water.

Crocodiles

Large and Larger

Today, while most crocodiles are large, the saltwater, or estuarine, crocodile is the biggest, with a length of up to 23 feet (7.01 m). This crocodile lives in estuaries where tidal rivers meet the sea. It can tip the scales at more than a ton (907.18 kg) in weight. Unlike most crocodiles, saltwater crocodiles can exist in both fresh or slightly salty water and live from 70 to 100 years.

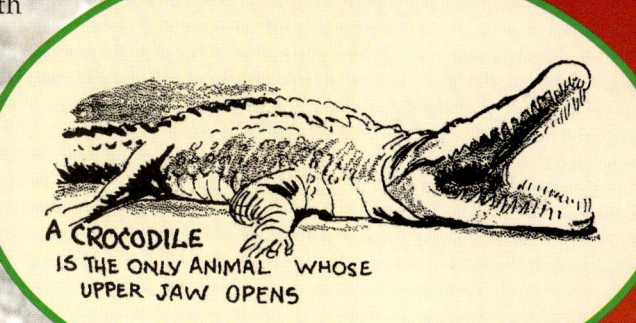
A CROCODILE IS THE ONLY ANIMAL WHOSE UPPER JAW OPENS

Crocodile Tears

Estuarine crocodiles can take in a lot of salt with their food, which consists of fish, crabs, and even larger animals such as turtles, birds, and mammals. To get rid of excess salt, they excrete it through the tear glands in their eyes. This is where we get the saying "crying crocodile tears"—meaning we think someone is only pretending to weep.

Note the scales that cover the crocodile's body.

Can a crocodile catch a running person? No, a crocodile can't move as fast as a person can on land—but, in the water, it can definitely outswim a person.

Crocodiles

Well-Ordered and Well-Watered

Crocodiles love hot spots and live in North and South America, Africa, Asia, and Australia. They are well-protected. Crocodile skin is made up of two layers. The outside layer is hard and hornlike and has scales that lie flat against the crocodiles' bodies. Bony plates, called osteoderms, form a kind of armor in the second skin layer beneath the scales. Crocodiles have 30 to 40 teeth in each jaw, which interlock when their mouths are closed. They have four-chambered hearts and highly developed senses.

Spending most of their time in the water, crocodiles lie submerged with only their eyes and nostrils showing. With their eyes and noses located on top of their heads, crocodiles can see and breathe while the rest of their bodies are hidden underwater. They can glide easily through the water and sneak up on their prey.

Crocodiles and alligators only eat about once a week because they can store fat in their bodies—primarily in their tails.

CROCODILES CAN JUMP 5 feet STRAIGHT INTO THE AIR!

Crocodiles are carnivores. This one may be in search of its next meal.

26

A Weighty Matter

Why don't crocodiles float? Adult crocodiles swallow stones, which settle in their stomachs and are never digested. Some scientists believe that crocodiles use the weight of the stones to keep their bodies below the waterline. The stones might also be used to help crocs break down their food by crushing and grinding it within the gizzard of the stomach.

Crocodiles

THE ZICK-ZACK BIRD PICKS THE TEETH OF CROCODILES.

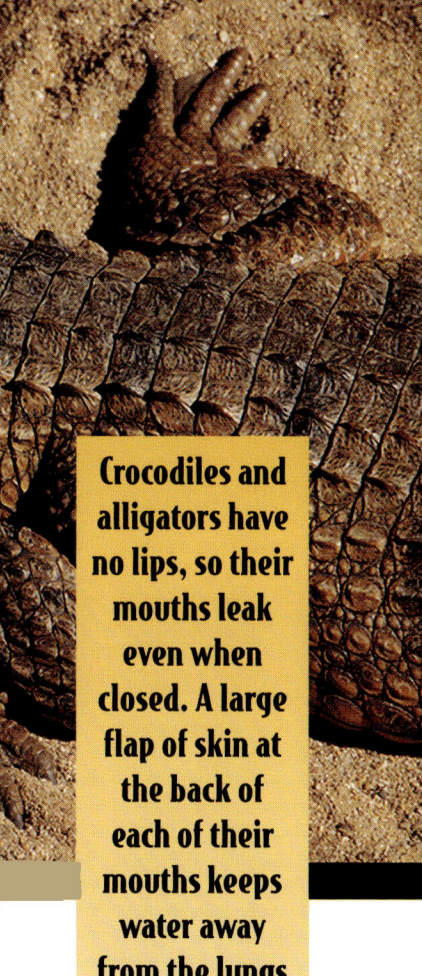

Crocodiles and alligators have no lips, so their mouths leak even when closed. A large flap of skin at the back of each of their mouths keeps water away from the lungs and prevents the crocs or alligators from drowning.

Crocodilians spend lots of time basking in the sun.

Hothead

Often, crocodiles will lie on the shore with their mouths open. This is not because they need to breathe but because they need to cool down. Like all cold-blooded reptiles, crocodiles must regulate their internal temperature. By opening their mouths, they allow cooler air to enter their bodies. If the weather is too cold or too hot, crocodiles will bury themselves in mud and hibernate or estivate—go into a deep sleep—during the winter or summer.

Crocodiles

Although they can be ferocious, crocodile parents are more attentive to their offspring than any other living reptiles.

Crocodiles may move clumsily on land, but they are awesome swimmers.

Deadly Enemies

The crocodile has few enemies, but those it has are deadly. Chief among them are humans. Crocodiles are on the endangered species list because people have hunted them to use their skin to make shoes, handbags, belts, and other items of clothing. Crocodiles are also in danger from their own kind. They will eat each other. Anaconda snakes lie in wait for crocodiles to come out of the water. When they do, the anacondas wrap themselves around the crocodiles and squeeze them to death. Large anacondas can swallow 6-foot (1.83-m) crocodiles. Disease and pollution also contribute to the deaths of crocodiles.

Notice the lower teeth that are sticking out above this marsh crocodile's upper jaw.

Alligators!

The word *alligator* comes from the Spanish word for lizard, *el lagarto*. Although alligators resemble crocodiles, alligators are more sluggish, preferring to remain in one spot or move slowly from place to place. They are found only in freshwater in the United States and China.

American alligators have broad snouts.

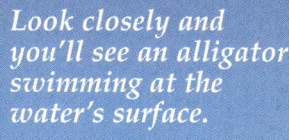
Look closely and you'll see an alligator swimming at the water's surface.

Alligators

It's the Teeth

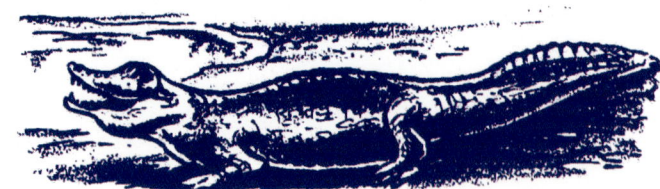

A crocodile is usually longer and heavier than an alligator and can outswim it, too. However, the best way to tell a crocodile and an alligator apart is to check the teeth. No teeth from the alligator's lower jaw can be seen when its mouth is closed. When a crocodile's mouth is closed, however, both upper and lower teeth are visible.

An alligator or crocodile may lose up to 3,000 teeth in its lifetime. New teeth are growing all the time to replace the lost ones.

The American alligator can reach 18 feet (5.48 m) in length.

See You Later, Alligator

Breeding season begins in April when an alligator starts courting. During this time, the male and female alligator may touch and rub their bodies together, bellow and grunt, and sometimes blow bubbles at each other in the water. A male alligator may mate with up to 10 or more females if he wins the battle against other males for the territory where a female is living.

A female alligator stays close to her babies for about a year. She protects the babies, but the little ones must find their own food.

Alligators

Baby Talk

Baby alligators are very chatty. They grunt, bark, and squeak to tell their mothers and the other baby alligators where they are. Young alligators form pods, groups that live together for up to two years. Pods may include alligators that are not related and are not the same age.

Older alligators make bigger noises. When they are mating or in danger, some alligators will raise their heads and tails out of the water and make noises that sound like heavy trucks thundering down a road.

THE AMERICAN ALLIGATOR, A RELIC OF THE DINOSAUR AGE, HAS REMAINED UNCHANGED FOR 200,000,000 YEARS AND WAS THREATENED WITH EXTINCTION BY THE LATE 1960s. BUT THE FISH AND WILDLIFE SERVICE REVERSED THIS SITUATION IN LESS THAN 20 YEARS!

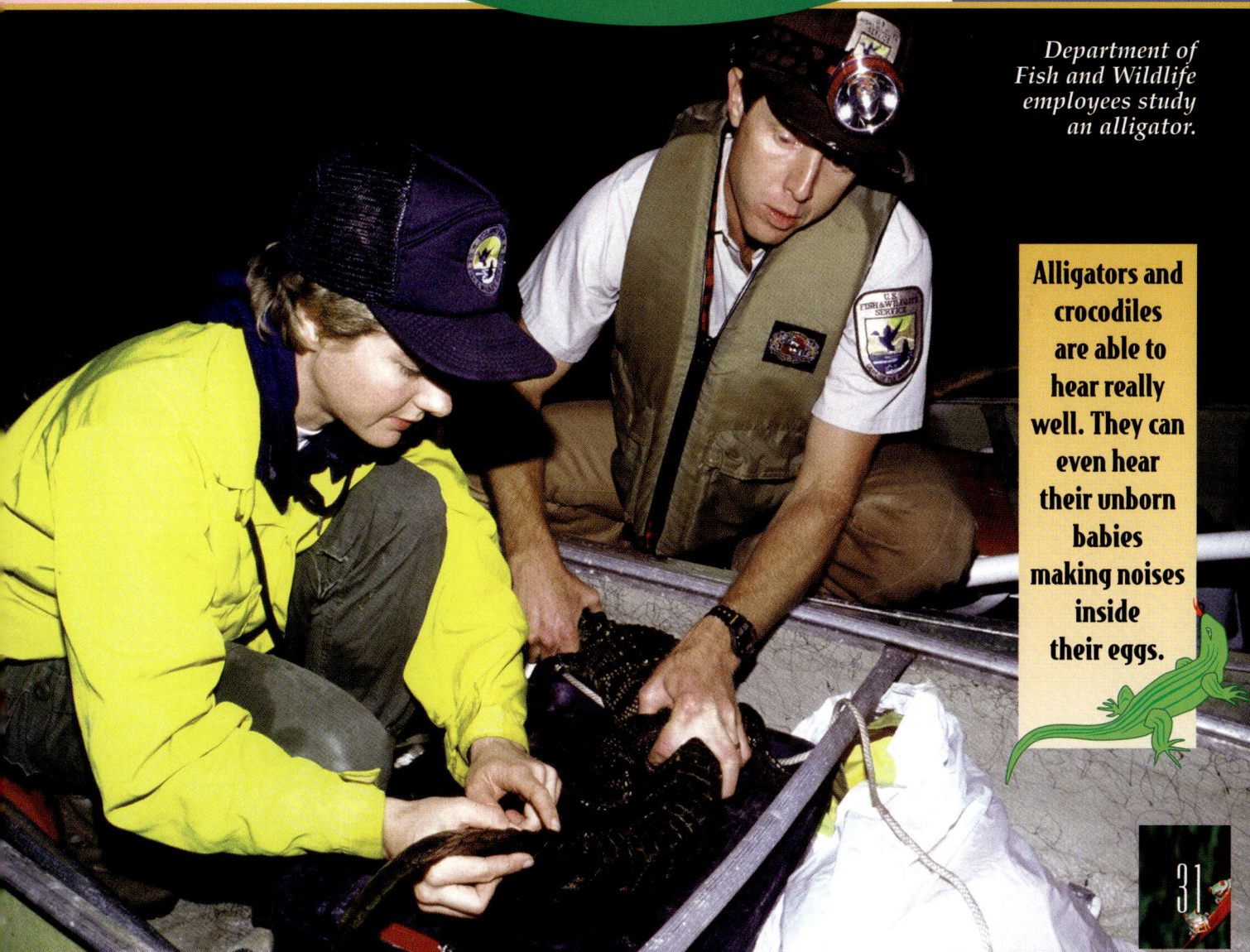

Department of Fish and Wildlife employees study an alligator.

Alligators and crocodiles are able to hear really well. They can even hear their unborn babies making noises inside their eggs.

Alligators

More Alligators

Other species of alligators include caimans, found primarily in Central and South America. One species of caiman is so adaptable that it has even been seen in polluted rivers near large cities. Another member of the crocodilian family is the gavial, also known as the gharial. Found in rivers from Pakistan to Myanmar, the gavial has a long, slender snout that is perfectly adapted for catching fish.

The male gavial scares off rivals by making a loud buzzing sound through a knob on its nose.

Some people compare the skin of white alligators to white chocolate. How sweet is that?

Like White Chocolate

When the alligator population in Louisiana appeared to be dying out, a private company decided to breed more alligators. There was nothing special about the alligators the company's team selected to have babies. To their surprise, however, some of these alligators turned out to be pure white with blue eyes. Normally, alligators are able to camouflage or hide themselves in their environment because of their color, but these alligators stand out. No one knows why the alligators are white. They are now basking in many aquariums and zoos.

Reptiles in Armor—
Turtles and Tortoises

The Shape They're In

Turtles and terrapins live in water while tortoises live on land, yet they all share the same body make-up. Cold-blooded with backbones, these reptiles are encased in protective shells. The part of the shell that covers their backs is called a carapace. A carapace is made of two layers: The inner layer is bony; the outer layer is made up of large scales called scutes. Some turtles have leathery skin without scutes, but most have these scales, which are made of keratin, the same protein we have in our nails and hair. The underside of the turtle is called the plastron.

The loggerhead turtle is called the dog turtle in Sri Lanka. That's because if you provoke it, the loggerhead might bite your finger off! The device on this turtle's back helps scientists track its behavior.

Instead of teeth, turtles have one big tooth—their sharp-edged jaws.

There are many different kinds of turtles but how they protect their heads is a major identifying characteristic. Side-necked turtles, found in South America, Africa, Australia, and nearby islands, fold their necks sideways under the top edges of their shells. Hidden-necked turtles, which live in North America, Europe, and Asia, pull their heads directly into their shells when threatened. Tortoises and sea turtles are also hidden-necked varieties.

The leopard tortoise is large. Some grow to more than 2 feet (60 cm) in length.

33

Turtles and Tortoises

How Slow Are They?

Turtles and tortoises have a reputation for being slow. Most times, this is true. If they had to walk a block in a city, tortoises would take about an hour to do it. Sea turtles, however, are among the swiftest of swimmers. While they may be slow on land, they almost fly through the water, using their hind feet to steer, and can reach speeds of up to 20 miles (12.4 km) per hour. Soft-shelled turtles can swim faster than most fish.

Galápagos tortoises can weigh more than 500 pounds (227 kg)!

THE GALÁPAGOS ISLANDS TORTOISE CANNOT BE IDENTIFIED AS MALE OR FEMALE UNTIL IT IS AT LEAST FIFTEEN YEARS OLD.

In the Galápagos Islands and the island of Aldabra, off the coast of East Africa, there are giant tortoises more than 4 feet (12.19 m) long.

This leopard tortoise is in front of a termite mound.

How Big?

Some turtles are relatively small. American mud turtles and musk turtles have shells that are less than 5 inches (12.7 cm) long. The tiny speckled cape tortoises of South Africa have a shell length of only 4 inches (10.16 cm). Yet, the leatherback sea turtle can weigh more than 2,000 pounds (907.2 kg) and have a shell length of 8 feet (2.4 m).

The Galápagos tortoise is the largest tortoise living today.

How Have They Survived?

Giant tortoises managed to survive over time—without speed, poison, or any other kind of defense. How? One way was to retreat to some of the most remote islands in the world where their enemies could not follow. Others became masters of crypsis—concealing themselves from predators by resembling their environment. Star tortoises of Asia, Madagascar, and southern Africa are able to conceal themselves because their pattern is undetectable in the deep grasses of the areas where they live.

Giant tortoises go to great lengths to regulate their lives. In some areas, they have eaten up all the green plants in the neighborhood and must trek long distances to find food. They wake at dawn to make this journey, always keeping an eye on the rising sun so they can time their return to shade before they become too hot and die. Being cold-blooded creatures, they must constantly adjust their temperatures.

Turtles and Tortoises

Lunchtime

Most turtles are omnivores; they'll eat almost anything. Tortoises, which move too slowly to capture other animals, are almost entirely plant and fruit eaters. Box turtles can even eat poisonous mushrooms without any distress.

Some turtles have worked out unusual strategies for catching their prey. By opening their mouths and wiggling a pink, wormlike part of their tongues, alligator snapping turtles attract fish. When fish swim inside the turtles' mouths to get the bait, the turtles snap their jaws shut and swallow the fish.

Alligator snapping turtles are the largest freshwater turtles in the world. They can grow to more than 30 inches (0.76 m) in length.

This alligator snapping turtle has its mouth open wide.

In 1774, a giant tortoise was presented to the ruler of Tonga by the explorer Captain James Cook. The tortoise was believed to be more than 200 years old and had survived fire, being run over, and being stomped on by a horse.

Turtles and Tortoises

Turtle Love

Some male turtles nip at the females' shells or necks, or bob or swing their heads over the females' necks when they are ready to mate. The females are not always willing. Those who are not ready to mate will pull into their shells or try to escape. Female green sea turtles sometimes avoid males by swimming away or folding their hind flippers together.

Turtles may mate either on land or in water, but all lay their eggs on land. Most females bury their eggs in a hole in the ground that they dig with their hind feet. After the females bury their eggs, which can number up to 200, they leave, providing no further care for their young. If the eggs survive, baby sea turtles crawl out of the nest immediately after they hatch and plunge right into the sea. However, birds and crabs may eat the hatchlings before they can reach the water.

A Department of Fish and Wildlife employee examines a green sea turtle.

A green sea turtle propels itself powerfully through the water.

Turtles and Tortoises

Sun-Loving Turtles

While most turtles and tortoises move from sun to shade and back again to keep their temperatures constant, the desert tortoise is an exception. These creatures love hot, dry areas and make their homes under rocks and shrubs during the most intense heat. They also dig burrows in which to sleep deeply during winter hibernation and summer estivation.

The bog turtle is an endangered species that lives in wet meadows, pastures, and bogs.

Take a Breath

When sea turtles are active, they must surface every few minutes to take a breath. However, if they are not expending a lot of energy, they can store enough air in their lungs to go for two hours without breathing. Turtles cannot move their ribs in and out to take in or expel air because their ribs are part of their shells. Instead, turtles expand or contract their muscles to change the amount of space inside their shells. When turtles expand their muscles, there is less space inside their shells and they can exhale. Contraction of the muscles allows turtles to inhale.

A Department of Fish and Wildlife employee studies a gopher tortoise.

Some sea turtles migrate more than 1,200 miles (1,931 km) to find suitable nesting beaches.

SENSATIONAL SNAKES

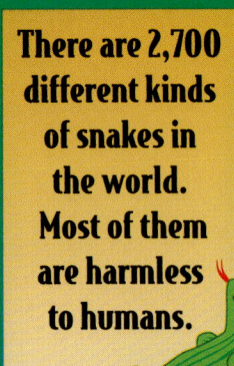

There are 2,700 different kinds of snakes in the world. Most of them are harmless to humans.

Black mambas are the fastest snakes alive. They can sprint 15 miles (24.14 km) per hour.

20/20 and Smell-O-Vision

Snakes are remarkable reptiles. Most snakes have good eyesight and an excellent sense of smell. They have round eyes that never blink because they have no eyelids. Clear "spectacles," which do not move, cover their eyes and protect them from dirt and dust. A forked tongue enables them to sense chemicals in the air, which are transferred to a special organ called the Jacobson's organ in the roof of the mouth. This gives snakes lots of information on the smells and tastes around them.

The northwestern garter snake has a blunt snout and usually has stripes along its body.

What a Body

The body of a snake is covered with scales that either have a center ridge or are smooth and flat. They are built to help the snake pull itself along the ground or in trees. A long snake may have more than 300 vertebrae in its spine, letting it coil and bend easily. A poisonous snake has two long hollow fangs that inject prey with venom. The larger the snake, the more venom it can produce in a single bite. When a poisonous snake's fangs aren't needed, the fangs fold back into the snake's mouth. A snake sheds its skin several times a year in a process called molting. This allows the snake to grow and replace old skin that is worn thin by rubbing, scraping, and crawling. Unlike other animals that shed, a snake sheds its entire skin all at once.

The scales of the Natal green snake can be clearly seen here.

Sensational Snakes

Snake Bites

Snakes are carnivores that eat small and large animals. Many are able to find their food by sensing the heat of animals near them. As long as the animal's body temperature is warmer than its surroundings, snakes can sense it. Some snakes have brightly colored tail tips. They hold up their tails and wriggle them. When the curious prey come close enough, the snakes grab a bite to eat. Boas, pythons, and anacondas are known as "constrictors." They kill by wrapping their strong bodies around their prey and suffocating it to death.

Snakes have no ears. Instead, they hear with their entire bodies, feeling sounds that vibrate through the ground.

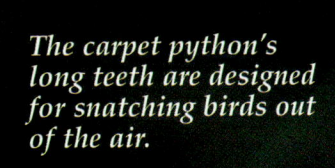

The carpet python's long teeth are designed for snatching birds out of the air.

An anaconda snake can kill and eat a full-grown caiman, but it may take the snake a week or more to digest it.

At Home with Snakes

Snakes live almost everywhere on Earth except for some islands and the North and South Poles. When snakes live in cold places, they hibernate during the winter. Sometimes up to 1,000 rattlesnakes will coil up together. Sea snakes are champion swimmers, flattening their bodies and tails against the water as they move. Shovel-nosed snakes slither under the desert sand to avoid the heat. If you're out at night in the desert, you might see sidewinders snaking their way across the sand. These snakes travel sideways, looping their bodies to keep from slipping in the sand.

The venomous sidewinder moves its body in an S-shaped curve.

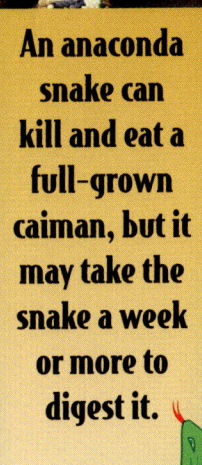

Sensational Snakes

The nonpoisonous emerald boa of South America blends into the greenery of the rain forest.

They Fly Through the Air

Many snakes live in trees. For some, this offers protection from their enemies. Seen from above, the dark tops of Cook's boa snakes blend in with the forest floor. From below, their light-colored bellies blend in with the sky. Flying snakes that live in the Asian jungle glide through the air by pushing out their ribs and holding their bellies flat until they look like ribbons. They steer through the air by twisting and turning.

Tree boas flop over branches in loops. If a choice morsel comes by, they straighten out and hurl themselves at the prey. Vine snakes wrap themselves around branches and dangle like harmless pieces of jungle vine. In one-third of a second, these snakes can snatch an unsuspecting bird or lizard.

Baby snakes get out of their eggs all by themselves. Each is born with a special little egg tooth to saw through the shell.

Rattlesnakes use their rattles to warn enemies to stay away. However, sometimes they bite without a warning rattle!

Eggs-actly

Some snakes, such as the young of the rattlesnake, are born live from eggs inside the mother. Other snakes lay eggs outside their bodies and leave them to hatch by themselves. Mud snakes lay their eggs in alligators' nests. Alligators will watch over the mud snakes' eggs as well as their own. Female king cobras remain with their eggs until they hatch.

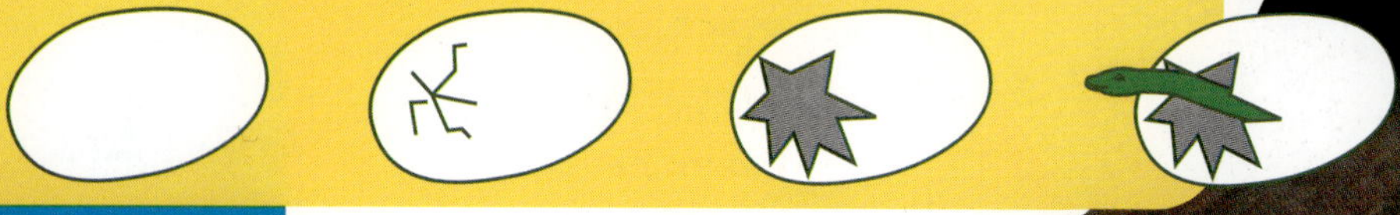

40

Sensational Snakes

The Pacific gopher snake is a common snake, found in grasslands and open areas in the northern United States.

Combat Dance

Male gopher snakes often fight for females but don't hurt each other. They stand up, twining themselves together, then try to push each other down. Again and again they wrestle until one gives up. Scientists call this the "combat dance."

Kingsnakes are active in the early evening. Their method for killing lizards, birds, small mammals, and other snakes is by constriction.

Rattlesnakes shake their tails to make sure larger animals don't step on them. The shaking causes their characteristic rattle.

Sensational Snakes

Life Savers

The colorful, but dangerous, coral snake feeds on lizards and other snakes.

It is sometimes difficult for ground snakes to get away from predators, so the snakes have developed many life-saving strategies. Harmless snakes often mimic or copy the skin patterns or colors of poisonous snakes. This is called crypsis. Milk snakes look like deadly coral snakes, but their stripes are arranged in a different order. Some snakes play dead when in danger. European grass snakes roll on their backs and lie still with their mouths open and their tongues hanging out. They know that dead snakes are not appealing to predators.

Some snakes have round tails that resemble their heads. Showing their tails when threatened, they hide their heads. When enemies attack their tails, the snakes can wriggle free and escape headfirst.

Before they bite in self-defense, small West Indian ground boas will squirt blood from their eyes.

The blunt-headed brown vine snake is a thin, mildly poisonous snake that closely resembles a vine.

Lizards:
Monsters, Speedsters, Dragons, and More

Living Large

Lizards are the largest group of reptiles. There are more than 4,300 species in a large variety of shapes and sizes. While lizards may look a little like salamanders, they have dry, scaly skin. Most have feet that end in claws, long tails, and ears that are visible from the outsides of their heads. Like snakes, lizards molt and shed their skin. Unlike snakes, their eyelids move and they shed their skin in small pieces. Lizards live in many different places, ranging from deserts to seashores.

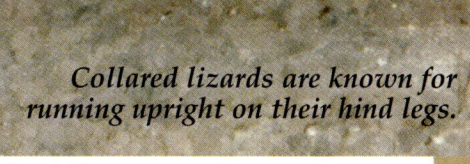

Collared lizards are known for running upright on their hind legs.

The Gila monster is one of two poisonous lizards.

Lizards have upper and lower eyelids. In some groups of lizards, the lower one is clear and protects the lizard's eyes from dust and thorns.

Only two kinds of lizards are poisonous: the Gila monster and the Mexican beaded lizard.

Monster Wrestling

Gila monsters spend more than 90 percent of their time underground in desert burrows. If they move about, it is usually at night when they track their prey by using their tongues to pick up scent particles. When they are active, they eat as much as they can and store it as fat in their tails. During the winter when they hibernate, they live off the fat. Male Gila monsters usually emerge from their burrows in the spring when they have monster wrestling matches with other males to compete for female mates.

Lizards

Oldest Lizard Speedster

The extinct lizardlike reptile, *Eudibamus cursoris*, lived 290 million years ago. It weighed less than a pound (0.4536 kg), was about 10 inches (25.4 cm) long, and could run at a top speed of around 15 miles (9.3 km) an hour. A few years ago, scientists in Germany discovered this little lizard, which might have been the first prehistoric creature to walk on two legs. Although it usually moved about on all four legs, *Eudibamus* was able to tuck its front legs under its body and run on its two back legs for speed. The little lizard was a vegetarian, so it didn't need to be fast to chase down its dinner. Scientists think it needed to be swift, however, to escape being the main course for a larger animal's meal.

The Komodo dragon, which lives only on the island of Komodo in Indonesia, grows to over 10 ft. in length!

Here Be Dragons

It can be 12 feet (3.657 m) long and weigh up to 380 pounds (172.36 kg). If it bites you, the bacteria in its saliva might kill you even if its sharp teeth don't. It's the Komodo dragon! It lives on the island of Komodo, in Indonesia, as well as on a few neighboring islands. The Komodo dragon may have been discovered as early as the second century C.E. by Chinese explorers searching for pearls. When they returned to China, they drew maps and labeled the area "Here Be Dragons."

Modern naturalists "discovered" the lizards in the early 1900s. They found Komodo dragons thriving in a hot, harsh climate with sparse rain, in a land of steep hills, rocky ground, and shallow soil. Although these lizards can overpower and consume any animal on the island, scientists consider them a vulnerable species. Humans kill Komodo dragons and have caused their main prey, deer, to disappear from the islands. People have also cut down the trees the lizards need for shade to regulate their body temperatures.

THE KOMODO DRAGON

THE WORLD'S LARGEST LIZARD, GROWS UP TO 12 FEET IN LENGTH, CHARGES AT GREAT SPEED, AND HAS BEEN KNOWN TO DEVOUR HUMANS.

Catch Us If You Can

Some lizards are experts in avoiding their predators or in standing up to them. Collared lizards can quickly scurry away to escape from predators. Basilisk lizards, however, do something completely different from most—they run on water to escape! These lizards live on the forest floor near rivers or streams in Central and South America. When threatened, the basilisks have the ability to run on water as far as a quarter of a mile (0.40 km). How do they do it? The basilisks have light bodies and broad feet. Their hind toes have scales that propel them and act like skis. However, if basilisks slow down, they can sink. Then the lizards must swim to safety.

The blue-tongued skink threatens its enemies by puffing up its body, hissing, and sticking out its long, bright blue tongue. The frilled lizard has a scaly neck frill that looks like a giant collar. When the lizard tightens the muscles connected to its tongue bones, the collar stands up and the lizard opens its mouth wide to frighten predators.

Some lizards fool predators. If an enemy seizes a lizard's tail, the lizard breaks off the tail. It keeps wiggling, keeping the enemy occupied while the lizard crawls to safety. A new tail eventually grows to replace the original one.

THE BASILISK LIZARD OF SOUTH AMERICA CAN RUN ACROSS WATER!

A collared lizard suns itself on a rock. If an enemy appears, it can quickly escape.

Lizards

The shingleback skink's tail looks a lot like its head—the better to confuse its predators.

Lizards

Drinking It In

Spiked and spiny, the thorny devil is a lizard that lives in Australia. It eats only ants. Each meal consists of nearly 1,500 of the little creatures. What does the lizard wash them down with? A drink of water. It may wait quite a while before slurping the H_2O, though. The creature's body is decorated with sharp points. Dew, rain, and any other water are caught in the areas between the spikes and run down the lizard's body until the water gets to its mouth. This is how the thorny devil gets virtually all its liquid refreshment.

Some lizards rarely take a drink, like Mexico's worm lizard, the ajolote, which lives in the desert and burrows into the ground. Very often, they get the little water they need from their food.

The desert horned lizard can be seen basking in sunlight along roadsides. It gets the fluid it needs from the food it eats—especially ants.

The thorny devil is well adapted to desert life. The tiny grooves between the spikes on its surface allow moisture to spread all over its body.

46

The collared lizard, a member of the iguana family, jumps from rock to rock to chase its prey.

Lizards

The 411 on Iguanas

Some iguanas, like the marine iguana, are among the largest lizards in the reptile family. Some live in trees, some near water, and some in desertlike areas. Most iguanas are found in warm parts of Central and South America and on some islands. They range in size from 6 inches (15.2 cm) to 6 feet (1.8 m) long.

When iguanas fight, they use their tails as whips.

Lizards

Chuckwallas mainly eat plants. Their flat bodies allow them to hide in crevices when they sense danger.

Clever Chuckwallas

When a snake, bird, mammal, or even a bigger lizard is chasing the chuckwalla, it squeezes into the nearest crack in a rock and blows its body up to one and a half times its normal size. If the predator tries to pull the chuckwalla out, its scales snag on the rock, making a tough job even more difficult. If all else fails, the chuckwalla, like a lot of iguanas, can snap off its tail. The predator then may chase the wriggling tail, which skitters away from the chuckwalla.

Acrobatic Anoles

Green anoles are truly leaping lizards. The little creatures, up to 8 inches (20.3 cm) in size, have long, slender tails, and are extremely acrobatic. They leap from branch to branch and can change their color from green to various shades of brown, depending on their mood and location.

Although anoles are sometimes called "American chameleons," they are really members of the iguana family.

Lizards

True Blue . . . or Green

Male western fence lizards are also known as "blue bellies," because they have a blue patch on their stomachs. To impress female fence lizards at courting time, the males do push-ups, which show off their blue undersides.

On Espanola, probably the oldest of the Galápagos Islands, the marine iguanas are a reddish color rather than the usual shade of black. When mating season arrives, male marine iguanas change their tint from red to green. Marine iguanas are also excellent divers. Flattening their tails to propel themselves down, the iguanas can dive to a depth of 45 feet (13.7 m). There, they can snack on the algae and seaweed that make up their diets.

The marine iguana has a crest running down the center of its back.

The Tuatara

Having survived for over 200 million years, the tuatara is one of an ancient group of reptiles that were around long before dinosaurs. Today, it is found only on a few small islands off the coast of New Zealand. While the tuatara may look like a lizard, it is not. It has an unusual feature: a third eye in the center of its head that may be used as a homing device to locate the sun. The tuatara has the ability to live in cold temperatures and can tolerate minimal breathing activity. In fact, a tuatara can go for an hour without breathing. It may share a nesting burrow with seabirds. When the bird fishes during the day, the tuatara sleeps in the nest. At night, when the tuatara hunts for food, the bird rests in the burrow.

Tuataras live to a ripe old age— sometimes more than 100 years.

49

Lizards

Strong Medicine

The world's fastest reptiles on land are the spiny-tailed iguanas of Costa Rica. They have been clocked at 21.7 miles (13.48 km) per hour.

Some iguanas need to be fast since they are food for many species. Spiny-tailed iguanas are popular with people living in rural areas. They believe that eating the flesh of these iguanas is good "medicine" and will make them strong. Green iguanas of Central and South America, which live in trees, are farmed for food. These iguanas are known by their nickname—"chicken of the tree."

Cactus for One

An iguana may eat plants, insects, and other small animals—or anything else it can find, depending on its species and stage of life. The land iguana has the strangest diet. Its favorite food is the prickly pear cactus. The lizard chomps on the cactus fruit and leaves. It removes the spines by moving the cactus around in its mouth. Cactuses provide both food and liquid for the land iguana, which can go for up to a year without drinking a drop of water.

A land iguana is standing up to reach its favorite food—prickly pear cactus leaves.

If an iguana feels threatened, it will leap from a high tree to water below. It will press its limbs to the sides of its body and use its powerful tail to push itself across the water and escape.

Iguanas have good eyesight. They can even see in color.

50

Lizards

The fingers and toes of a chameleon are ideal for grasping branches.

Unlike other chameleons that lay eggs, the Jackson chameleon, which lives in Kenya, gives birth to a fully developed live baby.

When a male chameleon wants to attract a female, he will change into his brightest colors.

This chameleon's coloration is a good match for its surroundings.

Changeable Chameleons

Most people believe that chameleons can change their skin colors to match their backgrounds. Some can change colors in 20 seconds, but scientists have found that the little lizards change color according to light, temperature, and their moods. Chameleons are normally brown and green to blend in with the trees that are their homes. If a brown chameleon decides to bask in the sun, it may turn green because the lighter color will reflect the sunlight better. When a chameleon is cold, it will turn a darker color to absorb the heat more efficiently. Angry chameleons may turn red or yellow.

All chameleons have eyes that swivel separately. Chameleons can see in two directions at one time. Their long tails let them balance on tree branches. They catch insects with their long, sticky tongues.

Chameleons' eyes can move independently of each other, giving the lizards a wide field of vision.

Lizards

Gripping Geckos

Over 800 species of lizards belong to the gecko family. Most geckos are chatty. They can quack like ducks, bark like dogs, click, or screech. They are the only lizards that can make any sound other than hissing. Geckos are known for their ability to walk up and down walls and travel upside down across ceilings. The secret is in their feet. On the sole of each gecko foot are millions of tiny hairs. Weak electric charges in the hairs and on the surfaces create a kind of static cling that keeps the gecko from falling.

Geckos are usually found in tropical regions, never in cold places. Recently, some species of geckos have appeared in Texas. Naturalists believe they may have stowed away on ships coming to the United States. If so, insects should beware! Geckos not only munch on small flying insects but also gobble up cockroach eggs.

Geckos can move rapidly and are extremely agile. They can stick and unstick their feet 15 times a second. They can even hang from the ceiling by a single toe.

The frilled leaf-tail gecko has big, bulging eyes without eyelids.

Lizards

Looking at Geckos

Geckos vary in size and looks. The frilled-tail gecko, found in Madagascar, looks frightening, but it is harmless. Nevertheless, the local Malagasy people refer to it as *taha-fisaka*, or "devil."

The leopard gecko, which is among the largest of all geckos, grows to 8 to 9 inches (20.32 to 22.86 cm) long. Found in Iran, Pakistan, Afghanistan, and India, this gecko resembles a leopard in coloring—with black or brown spots. Unlike other geckos, the leopard gecko does not have the kind of feet that enable other geckos to climb.

Tokay geckos look harmless, but they are fierce biters. Once tokays sink their teeth into something, they hang on and let go only when they want to. Like other lizards, geckos will lose their tails when attacked to try and divert predators.

Geckos get around—climbing vertically and even hanging horizontally.

53

Lore and Legend

Myth Information

Amphibians and reptiles have been the subjects of many myths and legends. There is the story of the princess who kissed the frog, which then turned into a handsome prince. In Japan, frogs are considered good luck. Some Australians and Native Americans believe that frogs actually bring on rain because they make a lot of noise before rainstorms.

Hindu myths claim that the universe was held up by four elephants standing on a turtle's back. According to one Native American tribe, the turtle was the first animal created. At that time, the world was covered with water, and the turtle saved all the other animals from drowning by teaching them how to swim.

Myth Understandings

In ancient times, reptiles were honored and feared. Medusa, a monster from Greek mythology, had snakes for hair. Milk snakes got their name because people thought they glided into barns to drink cows' milk. Actually, the snakes were hunting mice.

Ancient Egyptians worshiped a god named Sobek that had a crocodile head. They dressed some crocodiles in gold and covered their legs with gold jewelry. When they died, crocodiles were mummified and buried in their own coffins.

An urban legend has it that New York City sewers are infested with alligators. Supposedly, baby alligators brought home as pets were later flushed down toilets and said to enter the sewer system. While the story sounds good, it has been proven to be false.

In ancient Madagascar, it was believed that crocodiles housed the spirits of tribal chiefs. A person thought to have committed a crime would be thrown to the crocodiles. If the crocodiles ate him, he was guilty.

In the late 19th century, Americans believed that eating alligator oil and meat would protect them from tuberculosis. There is no proof this ever worked.

More about Cold-Blooded Creatures

Amphibians and reptiles are fascinating creatures that have adapted their bodies and their habits to make the most of their lives. To find out more about these cold-blooded creatures, read some of the books below:

About Amphibians by Cathryn Sill. Peachtree Publishers, Ltd., 2000.

Alligators & Crocodiles by Karen Dudley. Raintree Steck-Vaughn, 1998.

Amphibian by Barry Clarke. Dorling Kindersley, 2000.

Crocodiles & Alligators by Seymour Simon. HarperCollins, 1999.

Extremely Weird Reptiles by Sara Lovett. John Muir Publications, 1991.

The Flight of the Iguana by David Quammen. Simon & Schuster, 1998.

From Tadpole to Frog by Wendy Pfeffer. HarperCollins, 1994.

How Do Frogs Swallow with Their Eyes? by Melvin and Gilda Berger. Scholastic, 2002.

I Wonder Why Snakes Shed Their Skin and Other Questions about Reptiles by Amanda O'Neill. Kingfisher Publications, 1998.

Komodo Dragon on Location by Kathy Darling. Lothrop, Lee & Shepard, 1997.

Outside and Inside Snakes by Sandra Markle. Simon & Schuster, 1995.

Peterson Field Guides: Reptiles and Amphibians by Roger Conant and Joseph T. Collins. Houghton Mifflin, 1998.

Pockets: Reptiles by Leo Vita-Finzi and John Mapps. Dorling Kindersley, 2003.

Pond & River by Steve Parker. Dorling Kindersley, 2000.

Really Radical Reptiles & Amphibians by Leslee Elliott. Sterling Publishing Co., 1994.

The Snake Book by Mary Ling and Mary Atkinson. Dorling Kindersley, 2000.

The Snake Scientist by Sy Montgomery. Houghton Mifflin, 1999.

Snap! A Book about Alligators and Crocodiles by Melvin and Gilda Berger. Scholastic, 2001.

SuperCroc and the Origin of Crocodiles by Christopher Sloan. National Geographic, 2002.

Turtles, Toads, and Frogs by George S. Fichter. Western Publishing Company, 1993.

What Is a Reptile? by Robert Snedden. Sierra Club Books for Children, 1997.

Glossary

Acanthostega An early amphibian that lived more than 360 million years ago.

ajolote A little lizard that looks like a worm, spends most of its time underground, and lives in Mexico.

amphibians The word comes from the Greek meaning "a double life." Most amphibians live the first part of their lives in water and the second part on land. Amphibians were the first animals with backbones to adapt to life on land. They have moist skin and no hair, scales, feathers, or claws on their bodies.

archosaurs The word means "ruling reptiles" and refers to the crocodiles, dinosaurs, and flying reptiles that dominated Earth 250 million years ago.

caecilians Amphibians that resemble earthworms but have a backbone and are either yellow or purple. Caecilians spend most of their time burrowing underground.

carapace The hard shell that covers all or part of the back of an animal. The carapace of a turtle is the shell that covers its back.

carnivores Meat-eating animals.

chameleons Small lizards that can change color according to their temperature, available light, or their moods.

cloaca The rear end of the digestive and reproductive systems.

crypsis The resemblance of an animal to its surroundings to avoid being seen. Some animals do this by modeling—imitating a nonliving object like a branch; some do it by mimicking live animals. For example, the milk snake mimics the appearance of the poisonous coral snake and is protected if predators do not realize the difference.

Cynognathus An ancient reptile the size of a wolf that had four legs and a short tail. It hunted other meat-eating animals.

ectothermic Ectothermic animals are those that are cold-blooded; their internal temperature changes with their surroundings. Ectotherms rely on the outside temperature and their behavior (such as sunning on a rock) to maintain a constant body temperature.

efts Young, immature newts.

el lagarto A Spanish phrase meaning "the lizard." It was used to describe alligators when the first explorers found them. Later, the two words became "alligator."

estivate Animals that estivate spend the summer in a deep sleep.

estuaries Estuaries are at the mouths of rivers where the current meets the sea's tide. There is more salt in an estuary's water than in river water.

estuarine Formed in the part of the mouth of the river where the current meets the sea's tide.

Eudibamus cursoris A small, plant-eating lizard that lived 290 million years ago. *Eudibamus* may be the first prehistoric creature to walk on two legs.

excrete To eliminate from the body.

Gila monster The Gila monster is one of only two poisonous creatures in the lizard family. (The Mexican beaded lizard is the other.) Gila monsters are black with a pattern of pink, orange, or yellow.

gizzard The muscular part of an animal's stomach in which its food is crushed and ground up.

hereditary A hereditary instinct is an idea or way of behaving that has been passed down through the generations from parents to children.

hibernate Animals that hibernate spend the winter in a deep sleep.

Icthyostega *Icthyostega* was the first four-legged fish. It lived 360 million years ago.

Scientists have also discovered that *Icthyostega* was one of the earliest amphibians.

Jurassic Period The period from 208 to 146 million years ago. Birds, flowering plants, and many dinosaurs developed and lived during that time.

keratin A protein that is found in both humans and animals. Keratin is present in horns, claws, hoofs, bills, nails, and hair.

larvae The hatched young of some animals that, at birth, are unlike the parents.

metamorphosis The changes an animal goes through when it adapts to a new environment. Tadpoles undergo metamorphosis into frogs when they develop lungs and grow legs, among other changes.

molting Molting takes place when an animal sheds its skin.

mosasaurs These ancient, giant, meat-eating reptiles lived in the water and were powerful swimmers.

mucous Mucous is a thick, slimy liquid. Many amphibians are able to produce mucous in their bodies to make their skin moist.

nictitating membrane A third eyelid that can be drawn across the eye to protect it while allowing the animal to see part of what's going on.

omnivores Animals that eat everything—both plants and meat.

osteoderms These are any bones that are sunk in the skin. They include the bony plates that are part of a crocodile's body.

pheromones Chemicals that animals release to attract each other during mating.

plastron The part of the shell that covers the lower half of an animal such as the turtle.

pods Pods are small groups of animals of the same species that band together.

predator An animal that captures and feeds on another animal.

radiant heat Heating that comes about because of a hot surface. An amphibian or reptile will enjoy basking in the radiant heat of a sun-warmed stone or rock.

regulate To control or adjust. Amphibians and reptiles have to regulate their temperatures, moving from cool to warm spots, because they are cold-blooded.

reverberations When sounds are echoed.

Rhamphorhyncus An early flying reptile that had a wide wingspan and long, narrow jaws.

Sarcosuchus imperator The name means "flesh crocodile emperor." Its discoverers found that *Sarcosuchus* was a huge, ancient, meat-eating crocodile that lived more than 110 million years ago. It had more than 100 teeth in its long jaw.

scutes Plates made of bone or horn that cover the outside of an animal.

snout The nose of an animal.

tuatara The last of an ancient group of reptiles that have survived for more than 200 million years. Tuataras have three eyes, can go for an hour without breathing, and are one of the longest-lived animals.

tympanum A thin membrane that is an external hearing organ for some animals.

venom Poisonous liquid that an animal, such as a snake, releases into an enemy.

vertebrates Animals that have a backbone or a spinal column. All amphibians and reptiles are vertebrates.

vocal sacs These sacs are located on either side of a male frog's throat and amplify his croaking.

Index

A
Ajolote lizard 46
Alligator snapping turtle 35
Alligators 21, 24, 26-27, 29-32, 40
American alligators 29
American mud turtle 34
Amphibians 4-18
Anaconda 28, 39
Anoles 48
Anura 8
Arboreal salamanders 17

B
Basilisk lizard 45
Black mamba snake 38
Blue poison dart frog 10
Blue-tongued skink 45
Boas 39-40, 42
Body temperature 51
Bog turtle 37
Box turtles 3
Brown vine snake 42

C
Cactus 49
Caecilians 5
Caimans 31, 39
California newt 15
Camouflage 31, 53
Carapace 33
Carpet python 39
Chameleon 51
Chuckwalla 48
Cloaca 15
Collared lizard 43, 45, 47
Common toad 5, 8
Constrictors 39, 41
Cook's boa 40
Coral snake 42
Crocodiles 19, 22, 24-28, 30
Crocodilian 19
Crypsis 35, 42
Cynognathus 19

D
Darwin, Charles 20-21
Desert horned lizard 46
Desert tortoise 35
Devil dog newt 15
Dinosaurs 44, 50

E
Eft 15
Eggs 11, 21-22, 34, 40, 53
Emerald boa 40
Estivation 27, 37
Estuarine crocodiles 25
Eudibamus cursoris 44
Europena grass snake 42
Eyelids, of lizards 43

F
Fangs 38
Fire belly newt 15
Flying snakes 40
Fossils 19
Frilled leaf-tail gecko 52
Frog eggs 11-12
Frogs 5-14

G
Galápagos marine iguana 20
Galápagos tortoise 34
Gavial 31
Gecko 52-53
Giant tortoise 35
Gila monster 43
Gills 16
Golden poison frog 13
Gopher snake 41
Gopher tortoise 37
Green iguana 50
Green sea turtle 36
Gulf coast toad 8

H
Hellbender newt 15, 18
Herpetologist 5
Hibernation 27, 37, 39, 43
Hidden-necked turtles 32
Horned frog 10
Human threat 13, 28, 44

I
Iguanas 47-50

J
Jackson chameleon 52
Jacobson's organ, in snakes 38
Jaws, of alligator 30
Jaws, of crocodile 25, 30

K
Kemp's Ridley sea turtle 22
King cobra 40
King snake 42
Komodo dragon 44

L
Larvae 7, 16
Leaf-folding frog 13
Leatherback sea turtle 34
Leopard gecko 48
Leopard lizards 21
Leopard turtle 32, 34
Lizards 19-20, 22, 43-53
Lizards as prey 40-41

58

Loggerhead turtle 32
Long-nosed snake 41

M

Marine iguana 20, 47, 49
Mating, of frogs 11
Mating, of salamanders 15
Metamorphosis 3, 7, 16
Mexican beaded lizard 44
Migration of turtles 35
Milk snake 42
Morelet's crocodile 22
Mosasaurs 19
Mud puppy newt 15, 18
Mud snake 40
Myths about amphibians and reptiles 54

N

Natal green snake 19, 22, 38
Newts 15
Nictitating membrane 9
Nile crocodile 24

O

Orange-eyed tree frog 11
Ornate horned frog 4, 9
Osteoderms 26

P

Pacific giant salamander 7
Pacific gopher snake 41
Pacific tree frog 11

Pheromones 15
Pods, of alligators 31
Poison, of frogs 12-13
Pterosaur 19
Pythons 22, 39

R

Rattlesnakes 39-41
Red hills salamander 5
Red-eyed tree frog 8-9, 14
Red-spotted newt 15
Reptiles 19-53
Rhamphorhynchus 19
Rough-skin newt 6

S

Salamanders 5, 15-18
Saltwater crocodile 25
Sarcosuchus imperator 24
Scales 19, 32, 38
Sea turtles 36-37
Shingleback skink 45
Shovel-nosed snake 39
Sidewinder snake 39
Skin 6, 13, 15, 19, 27, 38, 43
Slender salamander 18
Snakes 19, 23, 38-43
Soft-shelled turtles 34
Speckled cape tortoise 34
Spiny-tailed iguana 50
Star tortoise 35
SuperCroc 24

T

Tadpoles 7, 11-12, 17
Tail, of newts 15
Tail, of salamanders 16
Tail, of snakes 39-42
Thorny devil lizard 46
Tinker reed frog 12
Toads 5, 8-14
Tokay gecko 52
Tomato frog 14
Tortoises 19, 32-37
Tuatara 19, 22, 49
Turtles 21, 33-37
Tympanum 10

V

Venom 23, 38, 42
Vertebrates 5, 19

W

Waxy tree frog 13

West Indian ground boa 42
Western fence lizard 49
Western patch-nosed snake 40
White alligators 31
White's tree frog 9, 10

Y

Yellow-eyed salamander 16

Photo Credits

Ripley Entertainment Inc. and the editors of this book wish to thank the following photographers, agents, and other individuals for permission to use and reprint the following photographs in this book. Any photographs included in this book that are not acknowledged below are property of the Ripley Archives. Great effort has been made to obtain permission from the owners of all materials included in this book. Any errors that may have been made are unintentional and will gladly be corrected in future printings if notice is sent to Ripley Entertainment Inc., 7576 King's Pointe Parkway, Suite 188, Orlando, Florida 32819.

t=top
tl=top left
tr=top right
tm=top middle

m=middle
ml=middle left
mr=middle right

b=bottom
bl=bottom left
br=bottom right

Corel Images
Copyright page (t), (l), Page i (t), (b), 6 (t), 7 (b), 10 (l), 14 (t), (m), 15 (m), 16 (m), 17 (b), 18 (b), 40 (tl), (mr), 41 (tl), (b), 41 (tr), (mr), 42 (t), (ml), (bl), 43 (bl), 45 (b), 46 (t), 48 (t), (m), (b), 49 (t), 52 (t), (b), 53 (t), (r), (bl) 58 (t), 59 (t), (b) © Corel Images

Digital Vision
Page ii (b), 2 (l), 3 (t), (m), 4 (m), 5 (b), 6 (m), 8 (tr), (m), (b), 9 (tl), (b), (r), 10 (tr), (b), 11 (tl), (mr), 11 (b), 12 (t), (m), (b), 13 (t), (l), (b), 14 (b), 20 (t), 21 (m), 22 (b), 24 (b), 25 (m), (b), 26 (m), (b), 27 (m), 28 (t), (b), 29 (m), 30 (t), 32 (m), 34 (t), (m), (b), 35 (t), 36 (b), 38 (bl) 39 (t), (b), 43 (tr), 46 (b), 47 (b), 49 (t), 50 (t), (b), 51 (t), (m), (b), 56 (t), 57 (b), 58 (b), 60 (b) © Digital Vision

Ripley Archives
Page 32 (b) © Ripley Entertainment

United States Fish and Wildlife Service
Title page © David Vogel/USFWS
Page 2 (r) © USFWS
Page 3 (b) © John and Karen Hollingsworth/USFWS
Page 3 (l) © USFWS
Page 5 (t) © C.K. Dodd, Jr./USFWS
Page 6 (br) © Gary M. Stolz/USFWS
Page 21 (b) © Gary M. Stolz/USFWS
Page 23 (tl) © David Bowman/USFWS
Page 23 (tr) © Beth Jackson/USFWS
Page 29 (t) © USFWS
Page 29 (b) © Jerry Tollison/USFWS
Page 31 (b) © John and Karen Hollingsworth/USFWS
Page 33 (t) © Ryan Hagerty/USFWS
Page 33 (b) © Gary M. Stolz/USFWS
Page 35 (m) © Gary M. Stolz/USFWS
Page 35 (b) © Gary M. Stolz/USFWS
Page 36 (ml) © John and Karen Hollingsworth/USFWS
Page 37 (tl) © R. G. Tucker, Jr./USFWS
Page 37 (b) © Ryan Hagerty/USFWS

Original Color Art
Pages 7 (t), 19 (b), 20 (l), 24 (m), 44 (mr), 51 (b), 54 (t), (b) by Ron Zalme

Original Ripley's Believe It or Not!® Cartoons
Page 12 (l), 15 (br), 23 (br), 25 (tr), 26 (bl), 27 (tr), 30 (t), 31 (tr), 34 (m), 44 (b), 45 (t)
Used with permission of Ripley Entertainment Inc.